PICTOLOGY

Space Explorer

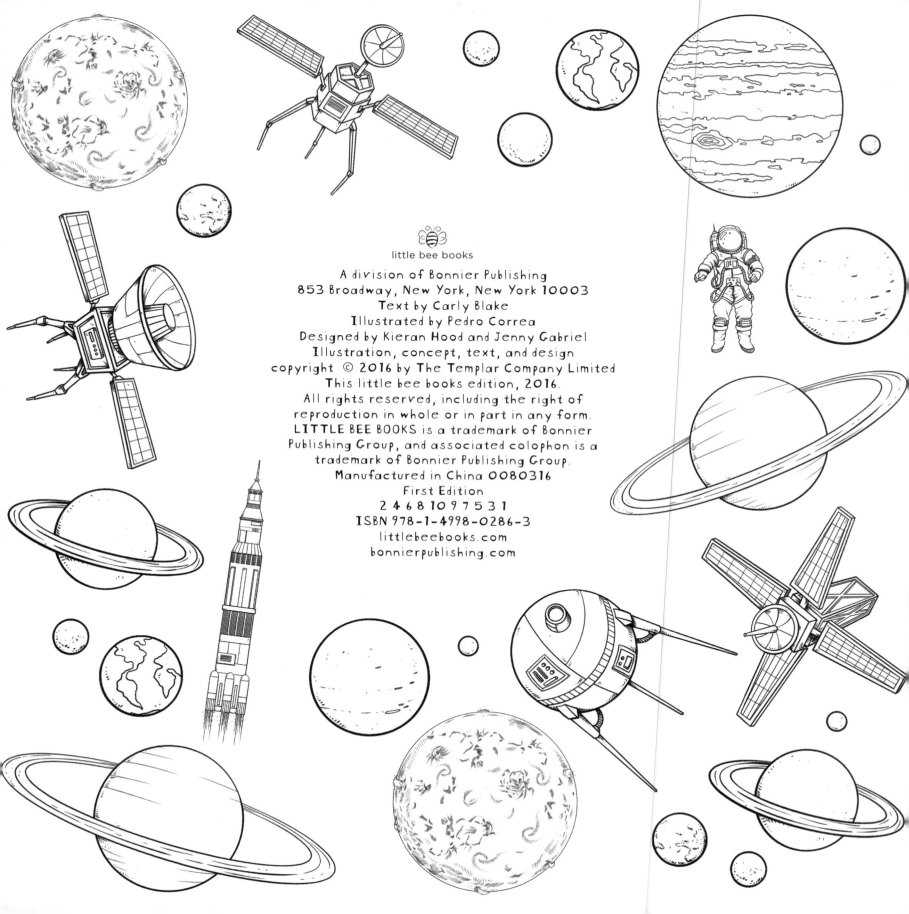

little bee books

A division of Bonnier Publishing
853 Broadway, New York, New York 10003
Text by Carly Blake
Illustrated by Pedro Correa
Designed by Kieran Hood and Jenny Gabriel
Illustration, concept, text, and design
copyright © 2016 by The Templar Company Limited
This little bee books edition, 2016.
Manufactured in China 0080316
First Edition
2 4 6 8 10 9 7 5 3 1
ISBN 978-1-4998-0286-3
littlebeebooks.com
bonnierpublishing.com

Pull out your favorite art materials.
Pore over each page.
Think, draw, and experiment.
Then make this book your own.

Art by Pedro Correa and

....

Write your name here.

Space Explorer

This is a unique introduction to mankind's exploration of space for aspiring artists and designers. Immerse yourself in inspiring patterns and motifs, spark your imagination with amazing facts, and then use your pen to bring these cosmic scenes to life. Every page offers something new to color, imagine, and draw.

Doodle and design.
Stop and start.
Color and create.
Make your mark.

Customize your stickers!

There are two pages of stickers at the back of this book. Design them, and then decorate the pages as you like.

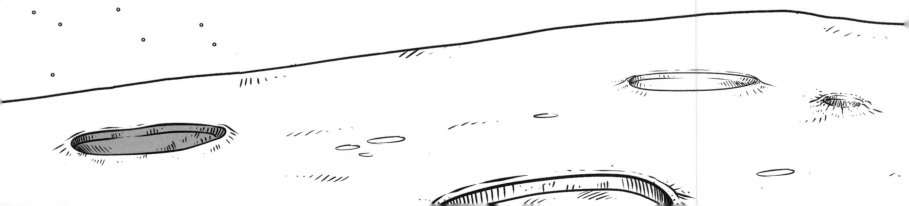

Things to look for:

Before you put pen to paper, look carefully at all the pages, taking in every detail. Can you spot these objects hiding on the pages? Check the ones that you find.

- [ ] **1** telescope
- [ ] **1** Cassini spacecraft
- [ ] **1** floating apple
- [ ] **2** joysticks
- [ ] **3** rockets

- [ ] **3** rovers
- [ ] **3** space shuttles
- [ ] **4** flags
- [ ] **7** astronauts
- [ ] **9** footprints

Map your own star patterns in the night sky by connecting the dots.

Scorpius
(Scorpion)

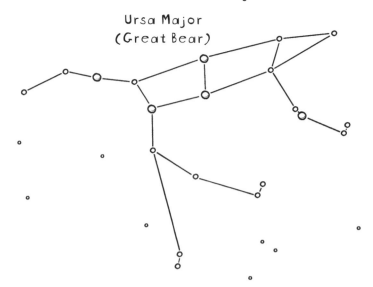

**Ursa Major
(Great Bear)**

**Sagittarius
(The Archer)**

Early stargazers saw patterns in the stars. They named them after mythical animals, people, or objects.

Earth is not alone in space. Use your brightest pencils to color all of the planets in the solar system.

Millions of asteroids zoom around between Mars and Jupiter. Draw some more.

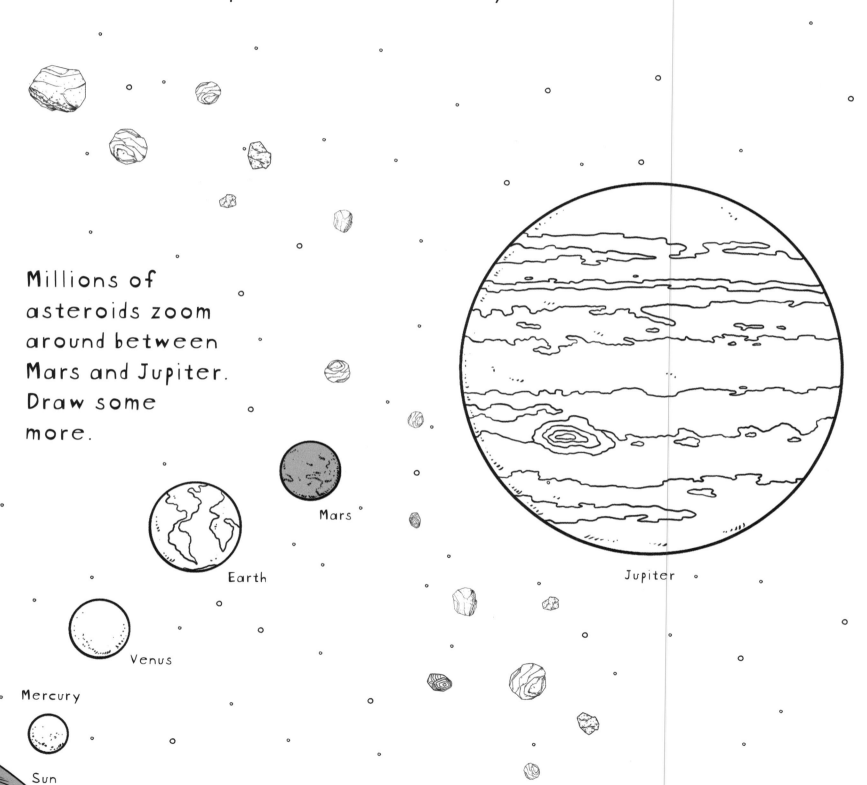

Mars

Earth

Jupiter

Venus

Mercury

Sun

Pluto
(dwarf planet)

Neptune

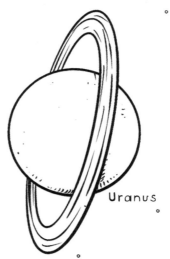
Uranus

Saturn

Mars, Mercury,
Venus, Saturn, and
Jupiter can be seen
from Earth at
different times
of the year.

The first spacecraft were sent into space in 1957. Design your own out-of-this-world spacecraft!

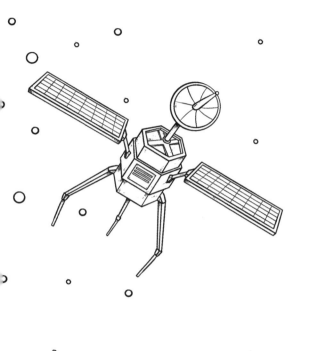

Sputnik 1 was the first artificial satellite in space. It looked like a metal ball with four long legs!

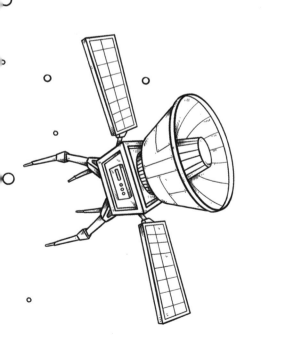

On July 20, 1969, Neil Armstrong became the first person to walk on the Moon. All around the world, people tuned in to watch....

Finish the television picture.

Color the space mission badges. Create your own cosmic designs for the missions you would like to go on.

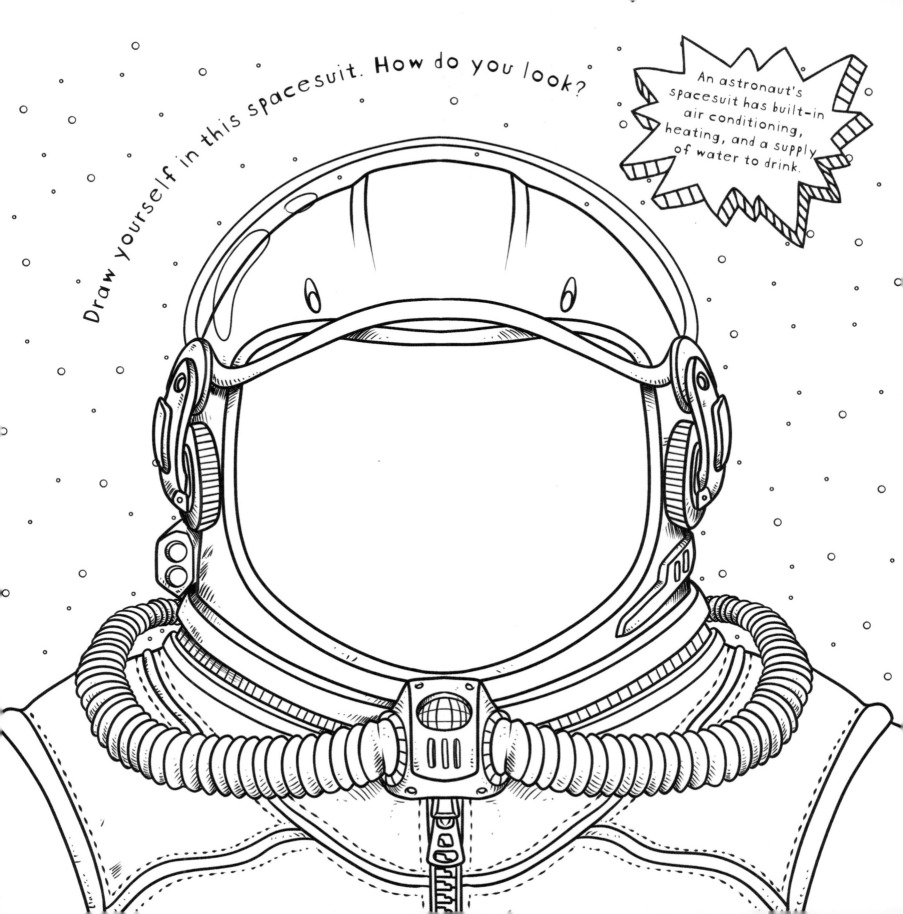

Draw yourself in this spacesuit. How do you look?

An astronaut's spacesuit has built-in air conditioning, heating, and a supply of water to drink.

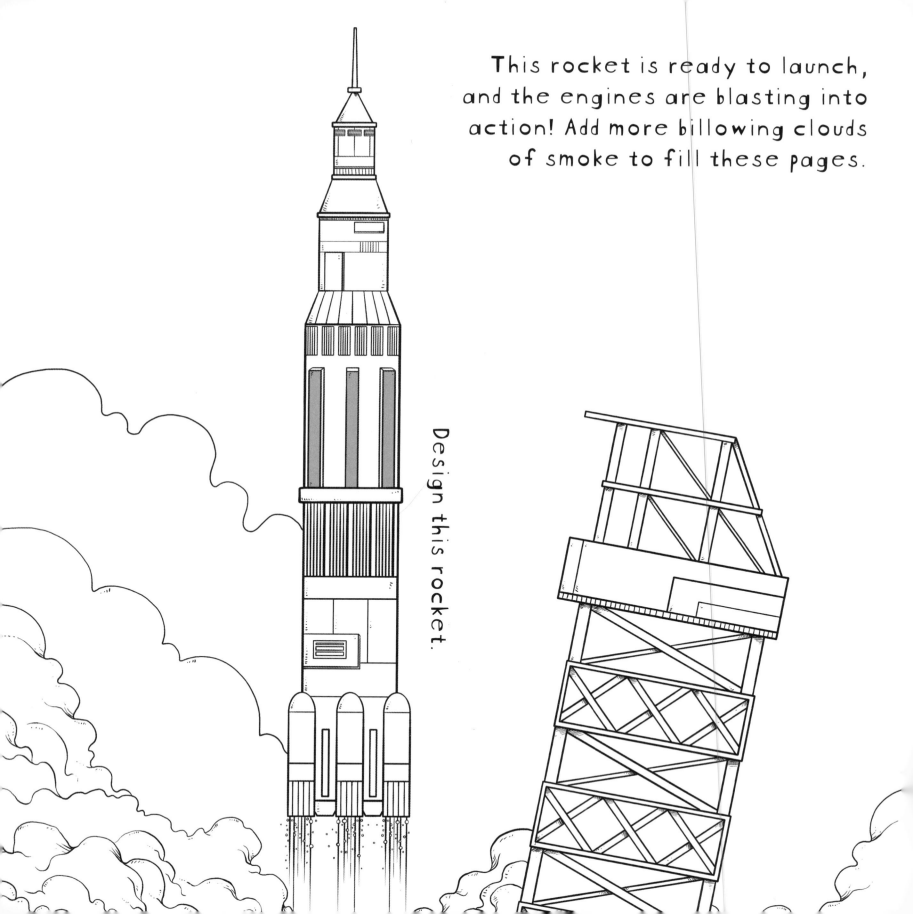

This rocket is ready to launch, and the engines are blasting into action! Add more billowing clouds of smoke to fill these pages.

Design this rocket.

Color the countdown.

3... 2... 1...
WE HAVE
LIFT OFF!

The Saturn V rocket, which launched the manned Moon missions, is the most powerful rocket ever built.

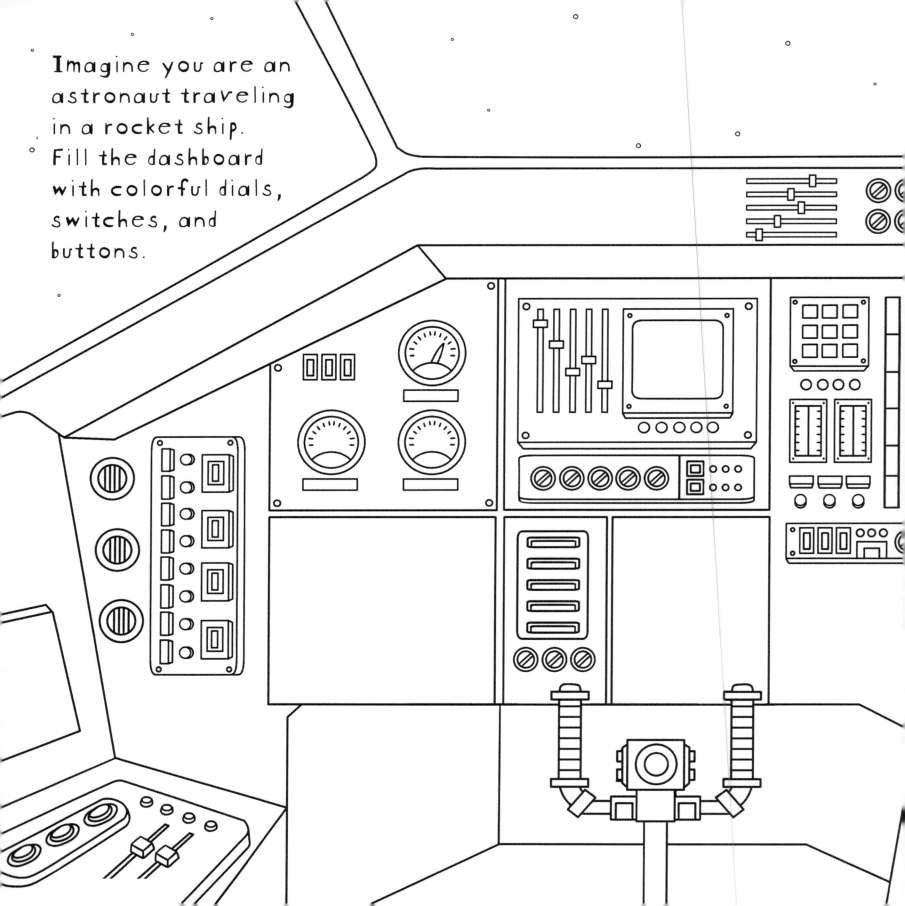

Imagine you are an astronaut traveling in a rocket ship. Fill the dashboard with colorful dials, switches, and buttons.

From launch, it takes 8.5 minutes for a rocket to reach space.

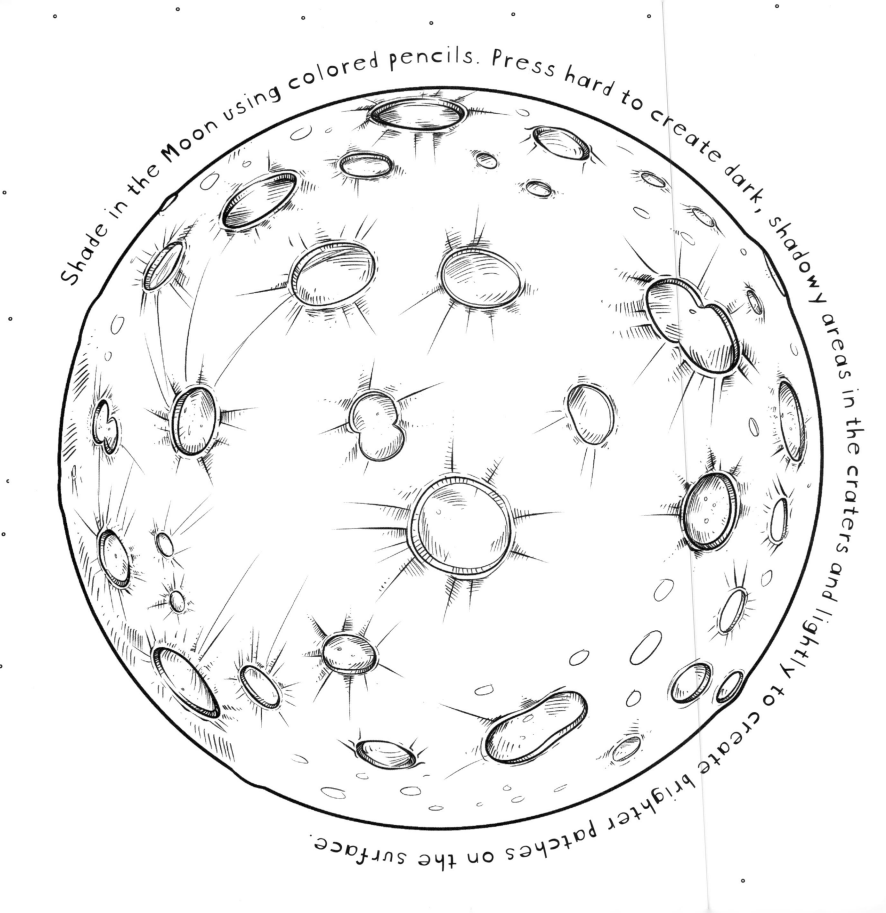

Shade in the Moon using colored pencils. Press hard to create dark, shadowy areas in the craters and lightly to create brighter patches on the surface.

The side of the Moon that faces away from Earth has hundreds more craters! How many can you draw?

We only ever see one side of the Moon. This is because the Moon rotates as it moves around the Earth.

A robot spacecraft touches down on the surface of the Moon.
Create the rocky, rugged landscape it's landing on.

In 1959, Luna 2 became the first spacecraft to land on the Moon.

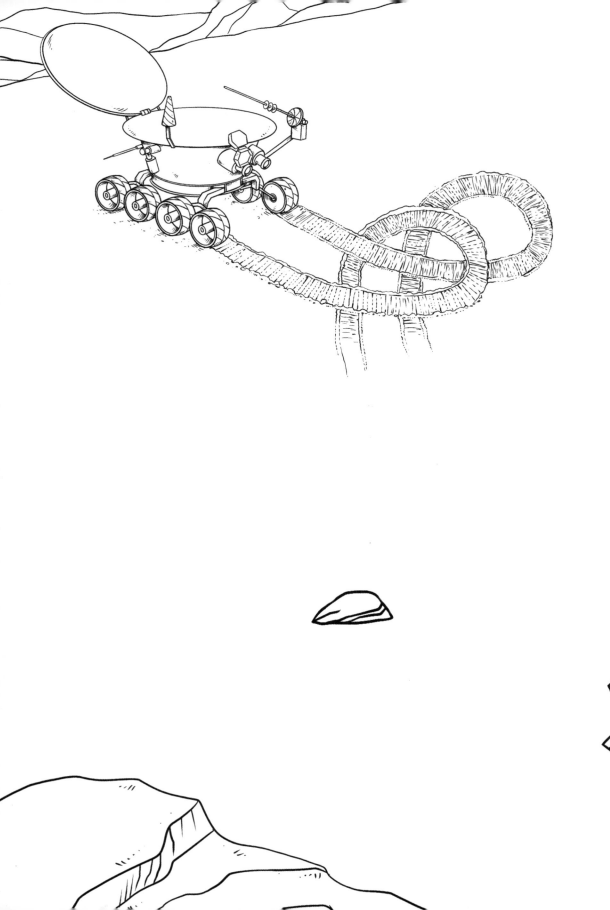

In 1970, Lunokhod 1 became the first rover to explore the Moon's surface.

Draw the path the rover has traveled from its spacecraft.

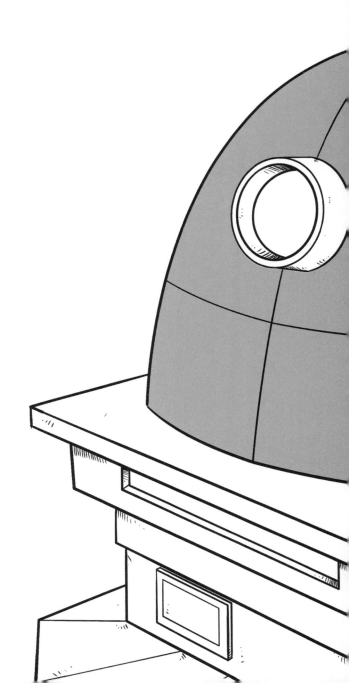

Color the famous scene from 1969—the first people to walk on the Moon.

Neil Armstrong and Edwin "Buzz" Aldrin spent 21 hours on the Moon and planted a flag on the surface.

Design your own flag.

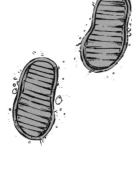

Twelve astronauts have walked on the Moon.
Sketch their tracks in the dusty surface.

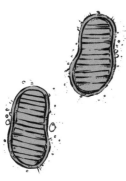
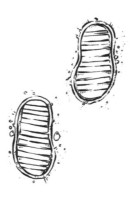
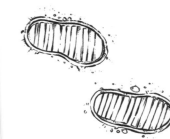

Add your own footprint on the Moon!

Place your foot on the page and draw around it.

Take a look at the Moon rocks brought back to Earth. Some have layers, some are shiny, and some are smooth.

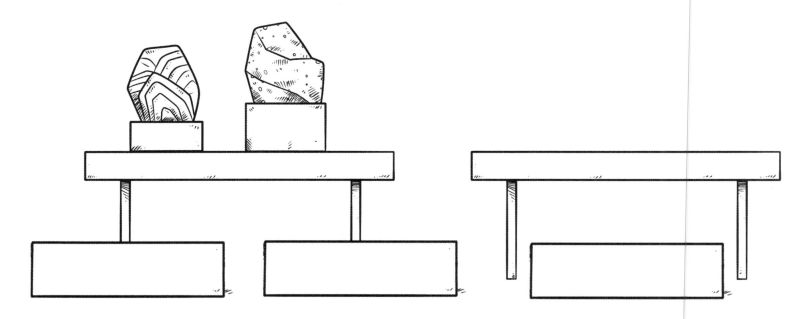

Fill the empty displays with your own extraterrestrial rock drawings. Label what planet they came from.

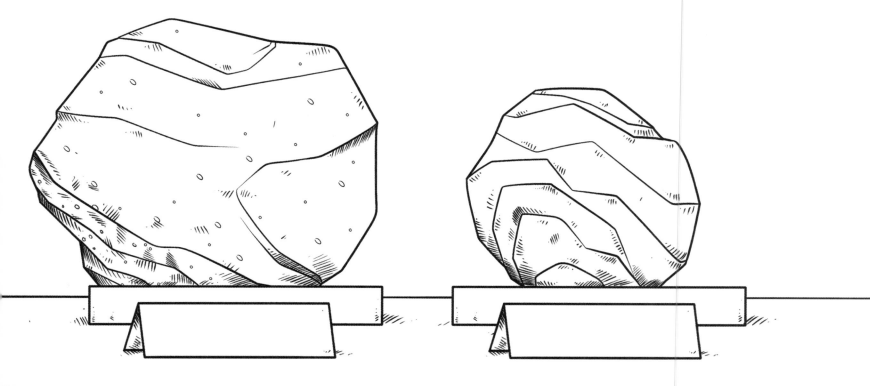

The largest rock brought back to Earth weighed more than 25 pounds—the weight of 11 pineapples!

You are standing on the surface of another planet.

You've spotted something on the ground that you want to bring back to Earth....

Draw it!

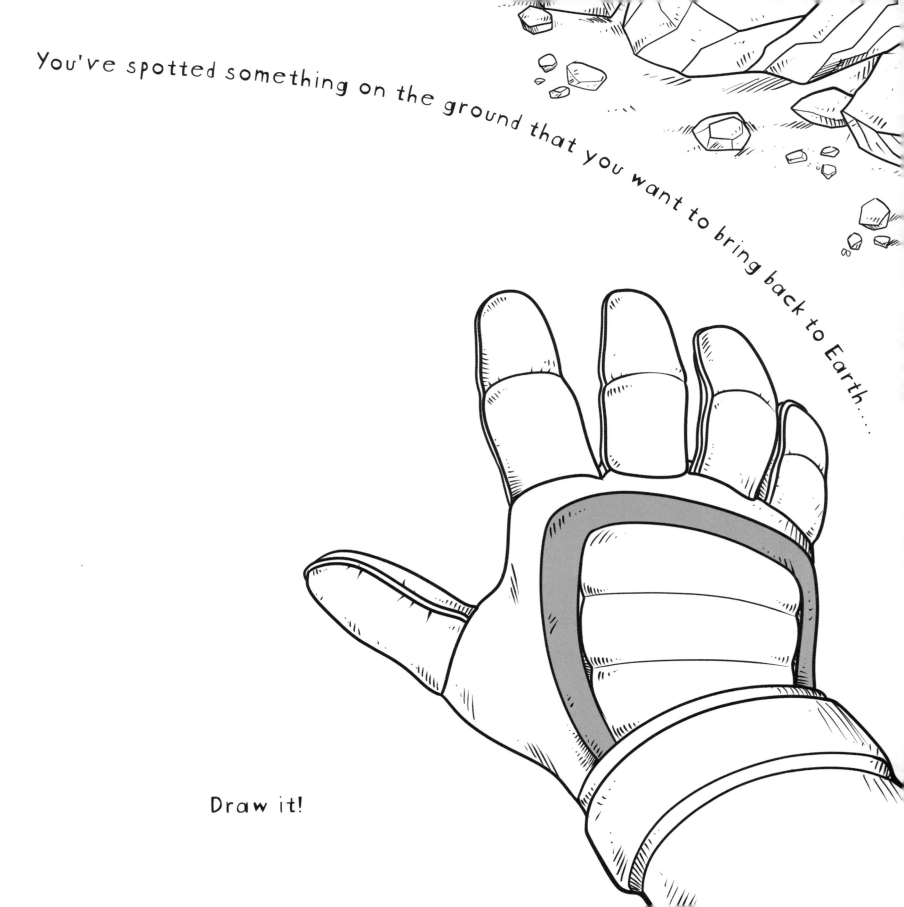

The view from the Moon looking back at Earth is a spectacular sight! Draw the countries of the world and color Earth blue and green.

Viewing Earth from the Moon, astronauts described the planet as looking like a "blue marble."

Can you see where you live?

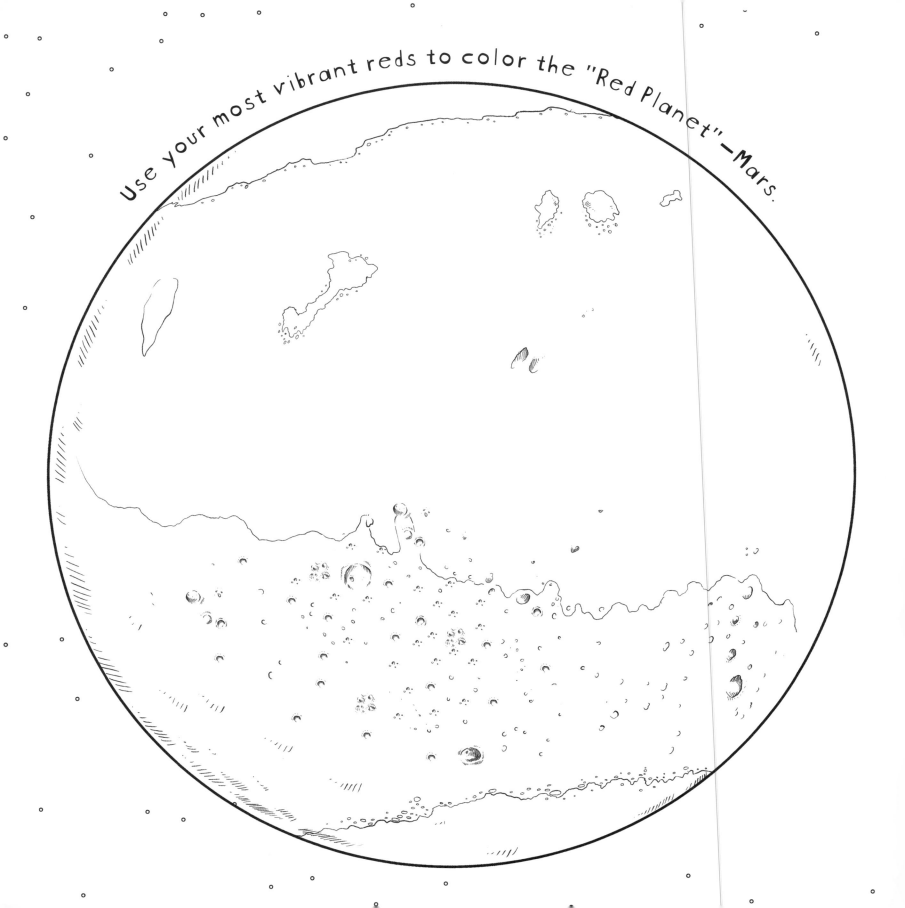

Fill this page with more spacecraft flying close to Mars.

More missions have been attempted to Mars than any other planet, but only half have been successful.

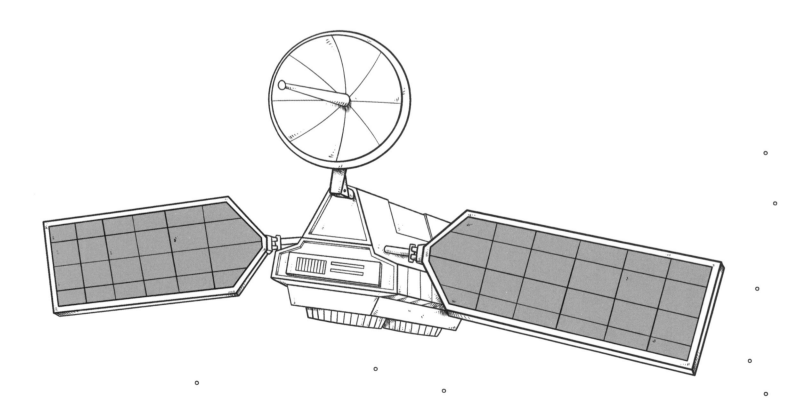

Equip this high-tech rover with extra gadgets to drill, collect, photograph, and measure its findings on the surface of Mars.

The car-sized rover *Curiosity* began exploring the surface of Mars in 2012. It may discover if life ever existed on Mars.

Curiosity

Four rovers have explored Mars.

Spirit

What name would
you choose for
your own rover
mission?

OPPORTUNITY

CURIOSITY

SOJOURNER

Color the page to bring these snapshots of Mars to life.

Olympus Mons volcano

Surface of Mars

Curiosity rover selfie!

Victoria Crater

Phobos, Mars's largest Moon

Fill the empty picture frames with your own scenes.

Many spacecraft have sent back fascinating pictures of Mars. One photo shows Olympus Mons—a 16-mile-tall volcano!

Color the International Space Station soaring high above the Earth. Use your stickers to add the spacewalking astronauts on the cables.

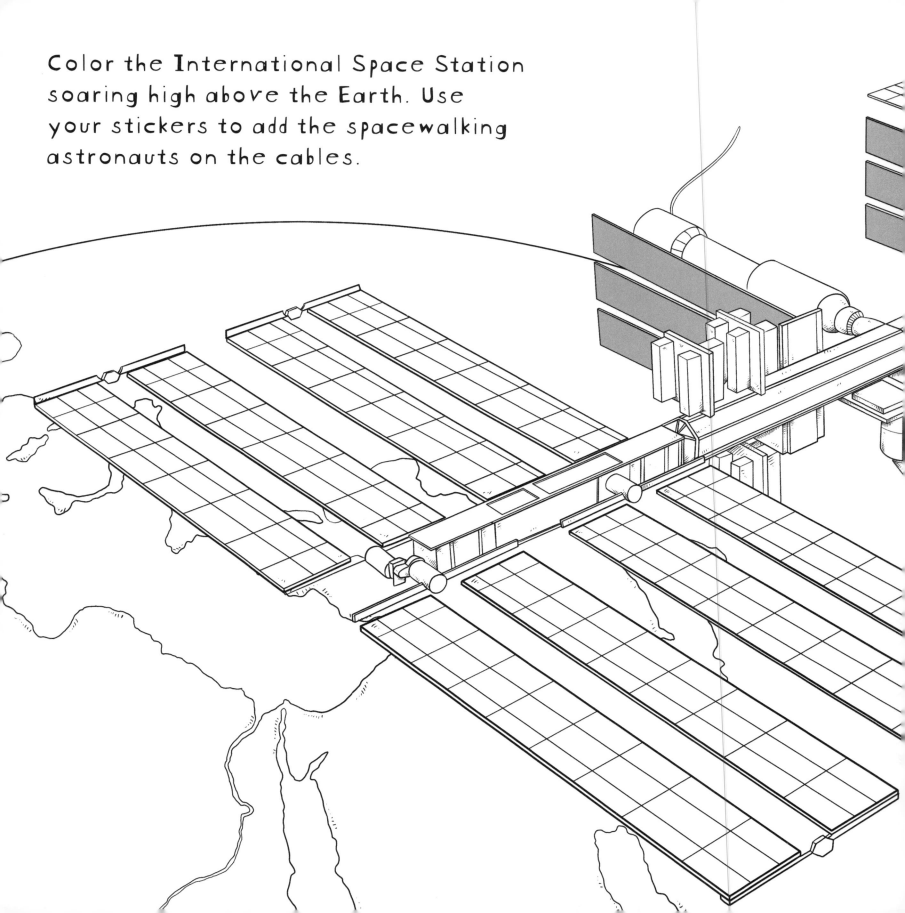

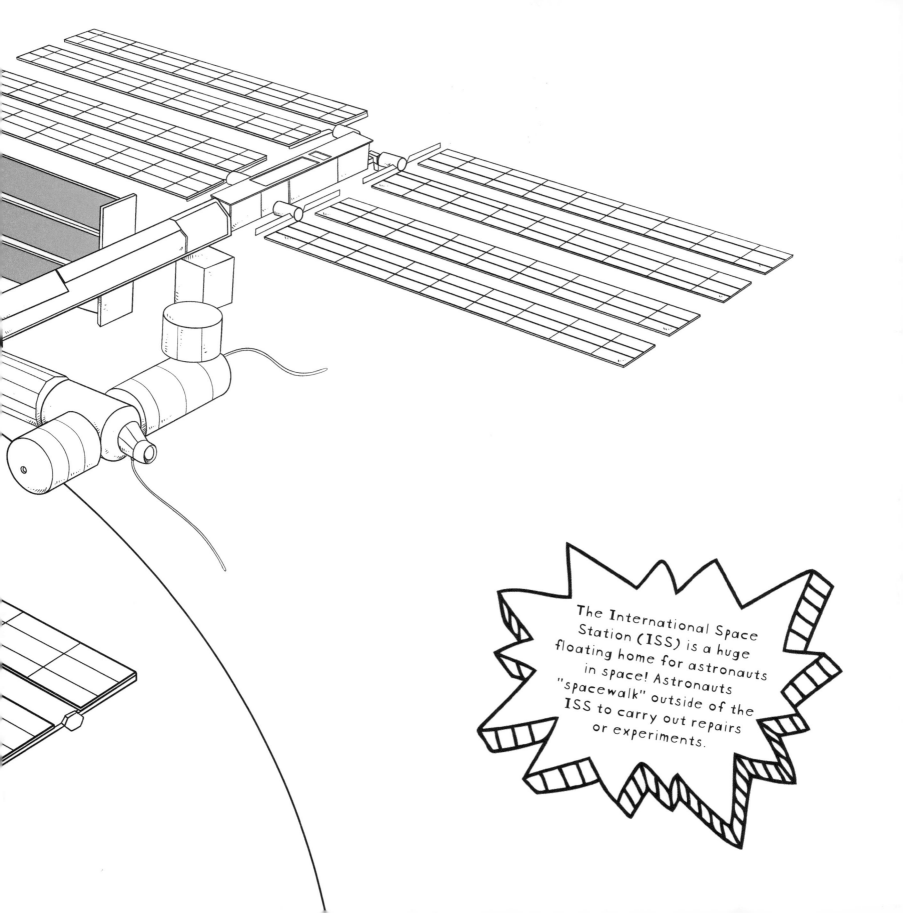

The International Space Station (ISS) is a huge floating home for astronauts in space! Astronauts "spacewalk" outside of the ISS to carry out repairs or experiments.

Astronauts— and anything else that isn't fastened down— seem to float in space.

In space, astronauts can move very heavy objects with just their fingertips because gravity is very weak.

Finish the scene inside the International Space Station. What else is floating around?

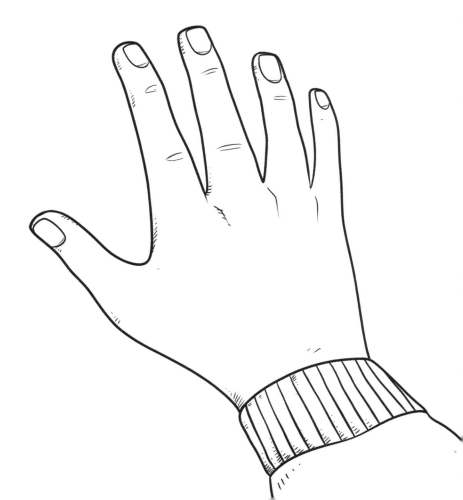

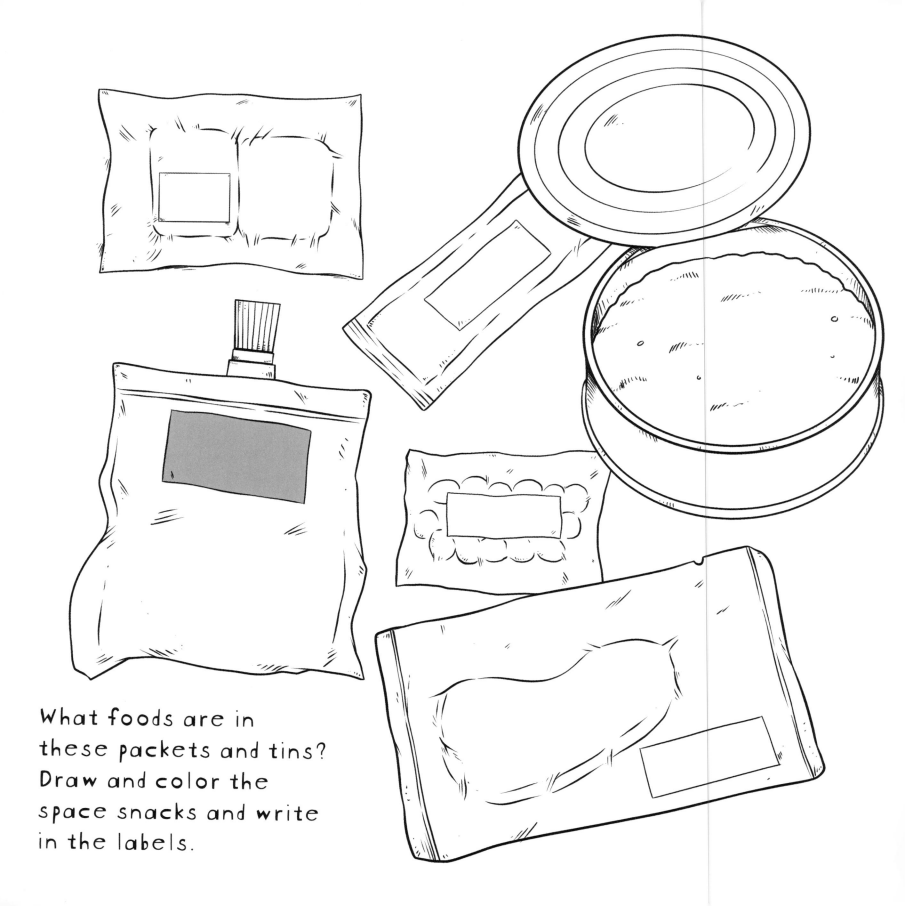

What foods are in
these packets and tins?
Draw and color the
space snacks and write
in the labels.

Design your own space meal.

Space food has to be specially packaged so that it can be eaten without flying away!

Watch out for the space debris! Can you find a path through the junk back to the International Space Station? Color the pages.

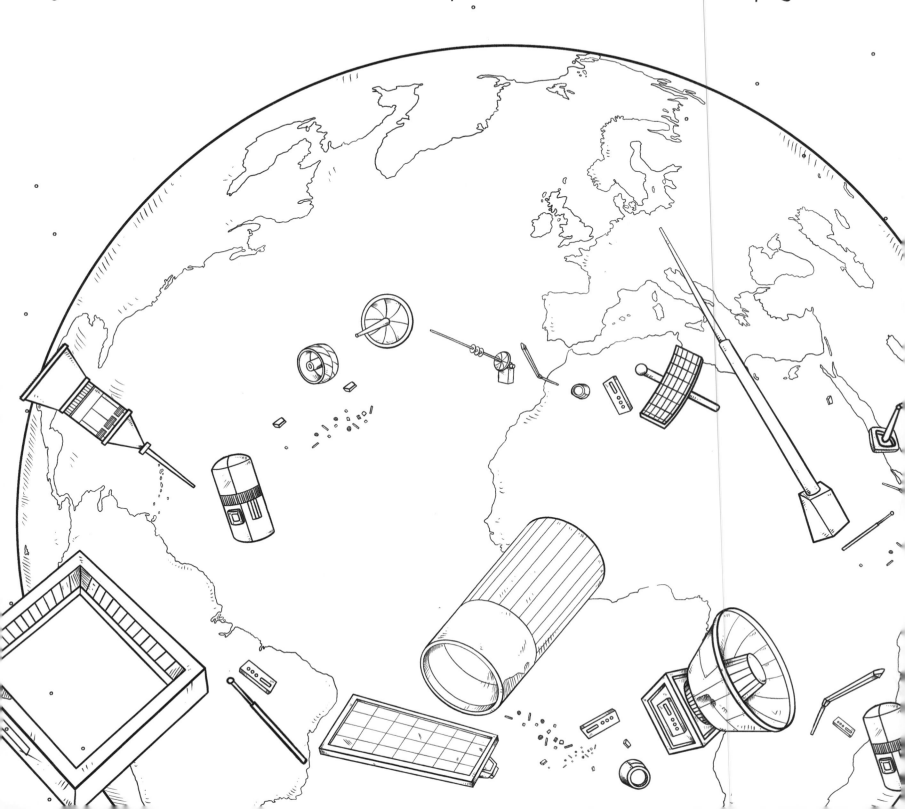

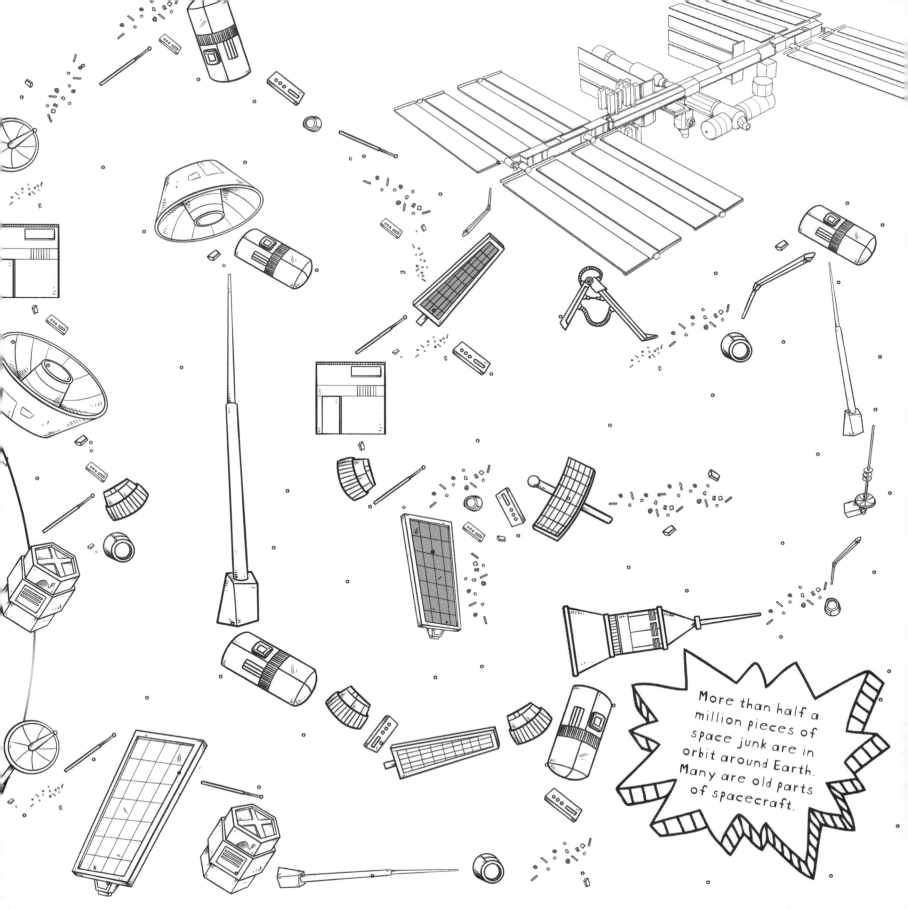

More than half a million pieces of space junk are in orbit around Earth. Many are old parts of spacecraft.

Welcome to the Spacecraft Hall of Fame! These long-distance machines have explored beyond Mars.

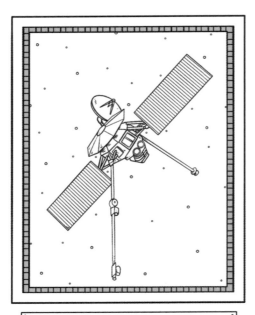

Mariner 10 (arrived 1974)
First spacecraft to visit the smallest planet, Mercury

Pioneer 10 (arrived 1973)
First successful mission to Jupiter

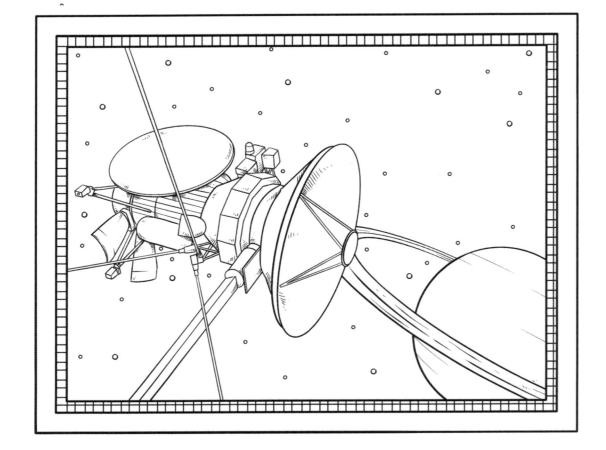

Cassini (arrived 2004)
Carrying out in-depth study of Saturn, its rings, and its moons

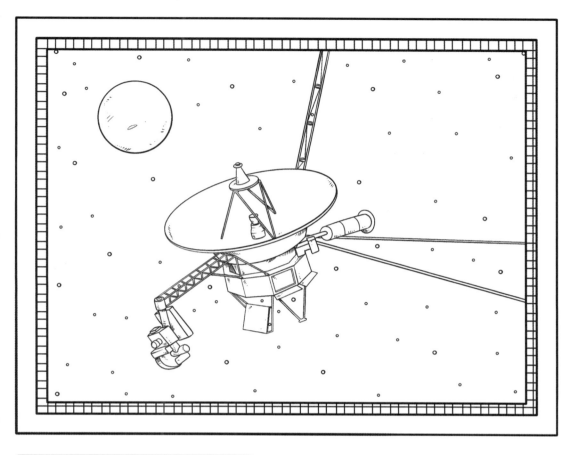

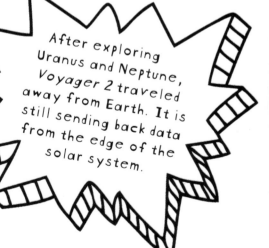

Voyager 2 (1986-1989)
Only spacecraft to explore
Uranus and Neptune

After exploring Uranus and Neptune, Voyager 2 traveled away from Earth. It is still sending back data from the edge of the solar system.

Venus Express
(arrived 2006)
Spacecraft began a
long-term study of Venus

New Horizons
(arrived 2015)
Only spacecraft to
explore Pluto

Design a spacesuit that could protect against the extreme heat and cold on Mercury, the closest planet to the Sun.

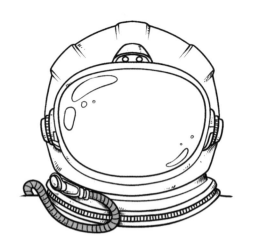

On Mercury it can be as hot as 800°F and as cold as -280°F! (Temperatures on Earth range from 134°F to -128°F.)

Craters of all shapes and sizes cover Mercury's surface.
Use a rainbow of color to fill them in.

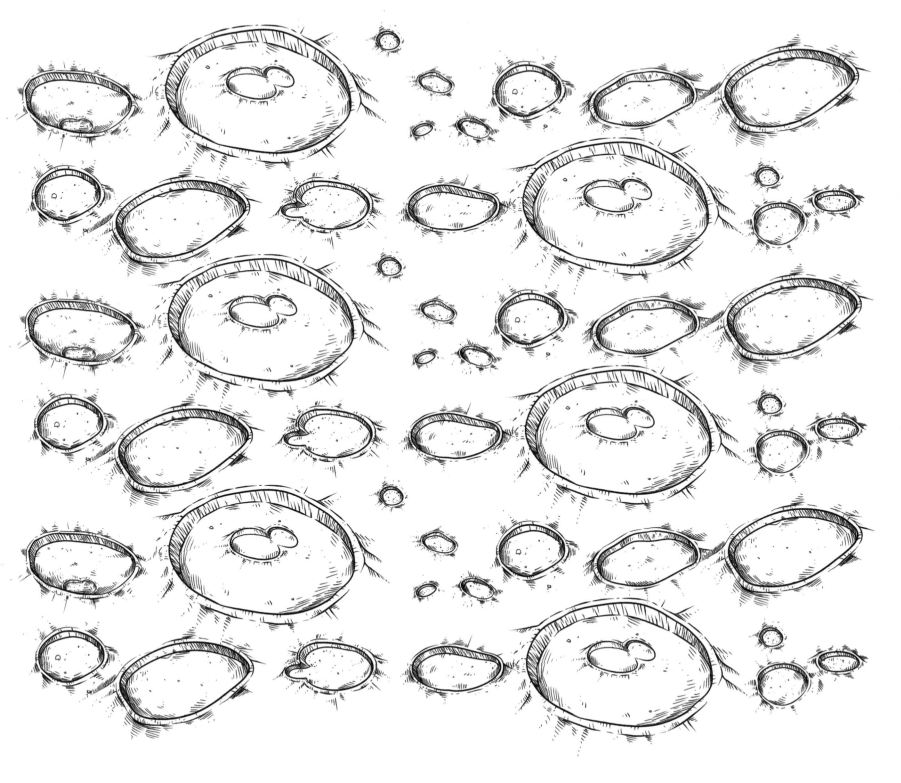

Make the volcanoes on fiery planet Venus erupt with lava and flames.

More than 30 spacecraft have visited Venus. Several landed on the surface, but they didn't survive for long in the harsh conditions.

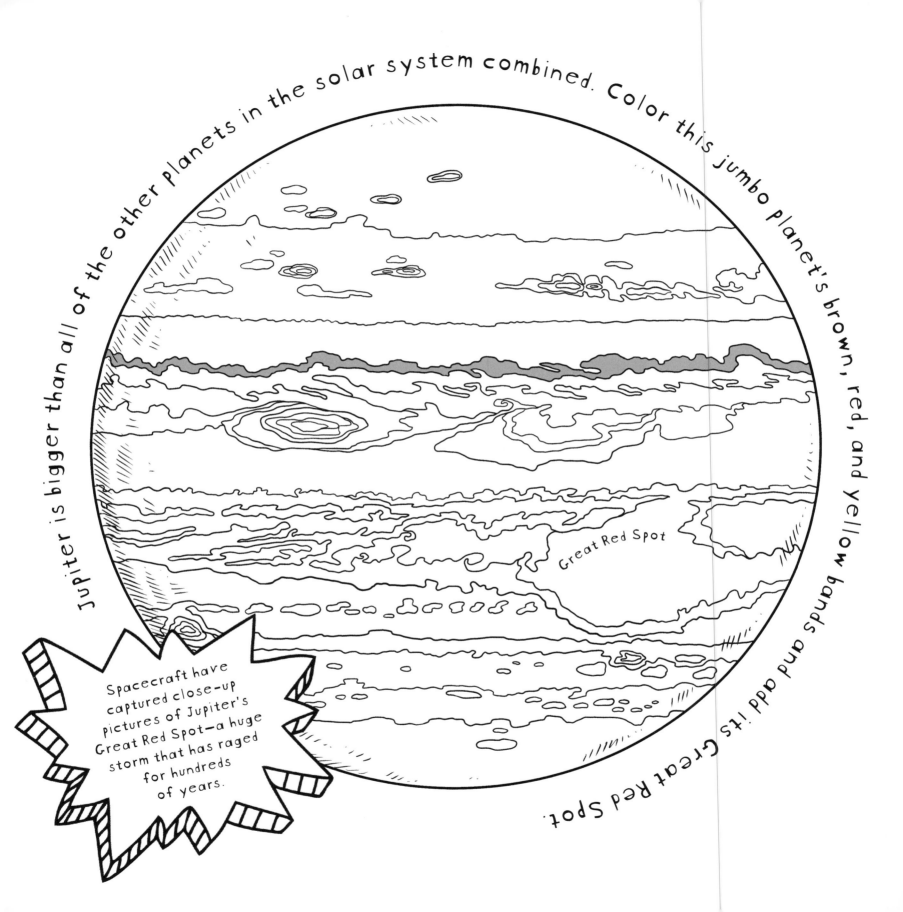

Jupiter is bigger than all of the other planets in the solar system combined. Color this jumbo planet's brown, red, and yellow bands and add its Great Red Spot.

Great Red Spot

Spacecraft have captured close-up pictures of Jupiter's Great Red Spot—a huge storm that has raged for hundreds of years.

Add Saturn's beautiful swirling rings,

stretching out around the planet.

Spacecraft that studied Saturn discovered its rings are made up of bits of ice, dust, and rock— some as small as sand grains, others as big as buildings!

Can you imagine an alien life form that might survive in the icy-cold atmosphere of Uranus? Draw it among the hazy blue-green clouds.

Uranus, the coldest planet in the solar system, was only discovered in 1781. Just one spacecraft has visited this distant icy world.

Color Neptune shades of brilliant blue. Surround the planet with **14** moons—one of them is shaped like an egg!

Voyager 2 arrived at Neptune in 1989 and sent back pictures of this dazzling planet. The gases in Neptune's atmosphere make it appear bright blue.

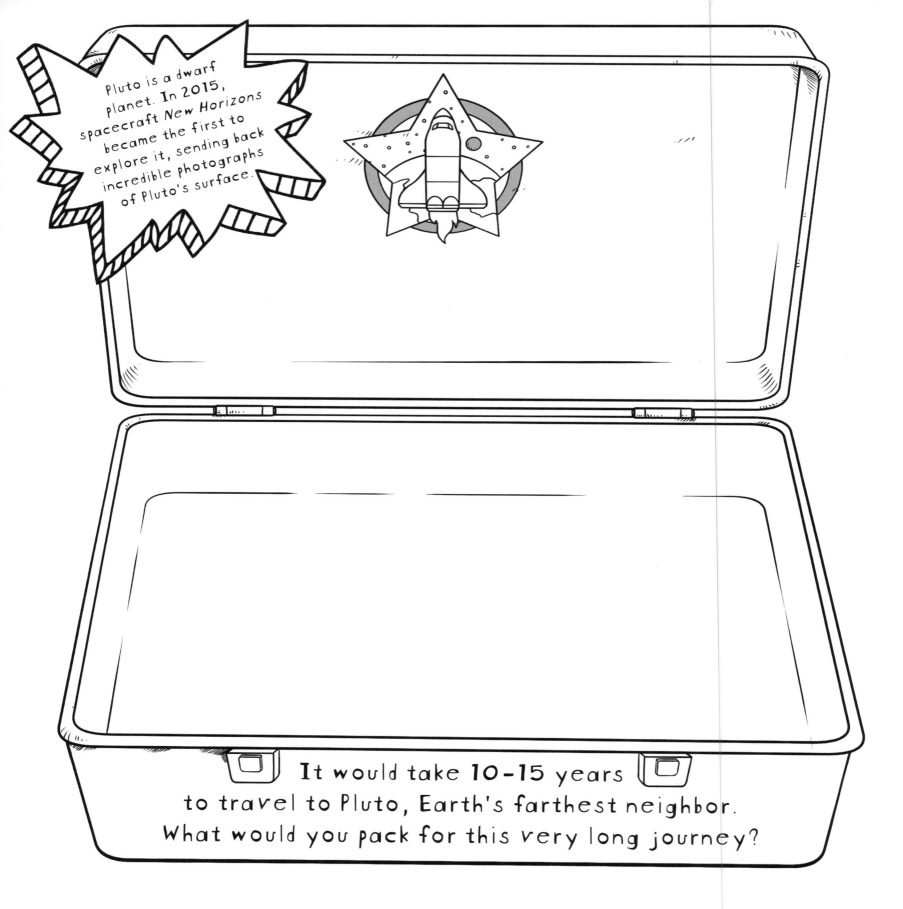

Pluto is a dwarf planet. In 2015, spacecraft *New Horizons* became the first to explore it, sending back incredible photographs of Pluto's surface.

It would take **10–15** years to travel to Pluto, Earth's farthest neighbor. What would you pack for this very long journey?

Use your brightest yellows, reds, and oranges to color the Sun.

Spacecraft designed to fly close to the Sun are equipped with thick heat shields to survive the blazing temperatures.

Complete and cosmically color this pattern of planets.

Color the comets zooming through space and add some more.

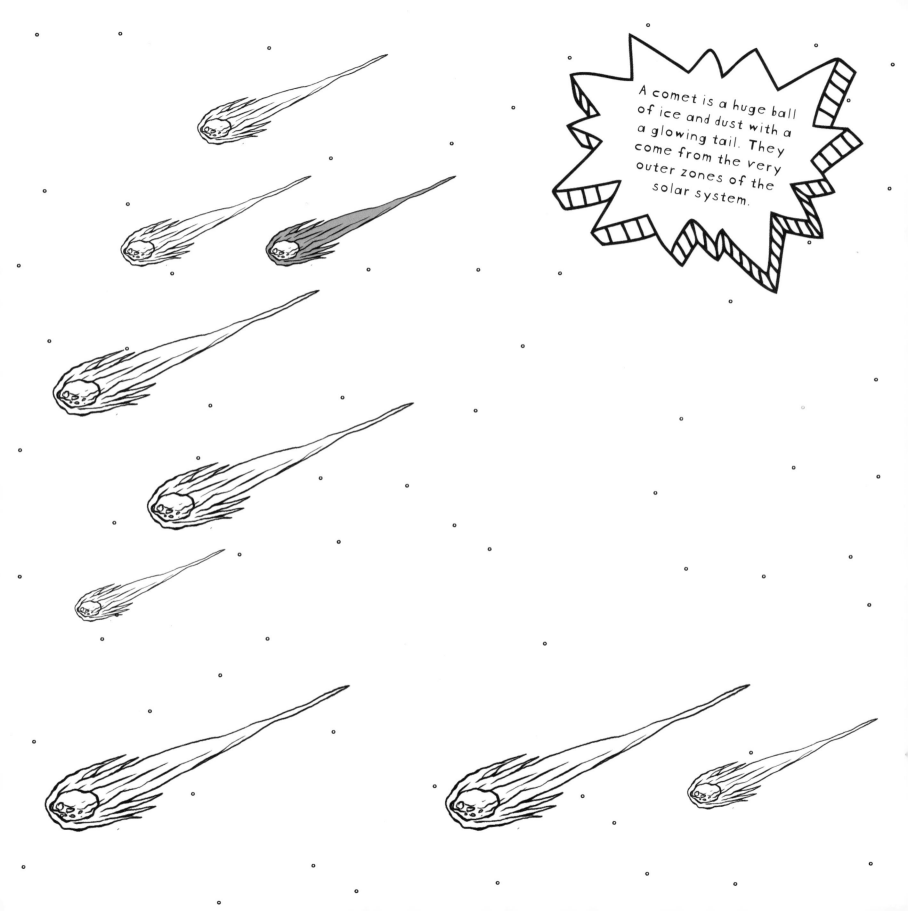

A comet is a huge ball of ice and dust with a a glowing tail. They come from the very outer zones of the solar system.

Design your own certificate from the Astronaut Academy. Write in your name and where you would like to explore!

Name: ....

Has completed their astronaut training and is certified to go into space.

Date certificate issued:

....

First mission departure date: ....

To explore: ....

Signed: ....

(Jimmy Galactic, Director of the Astronaut Academy)

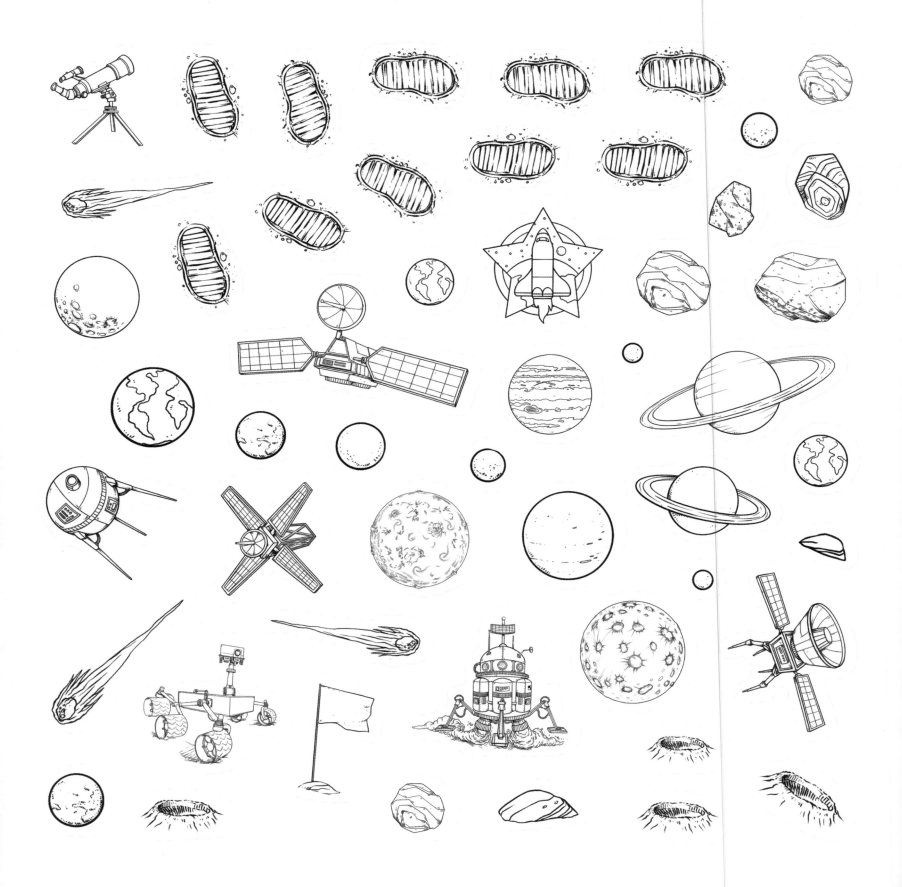

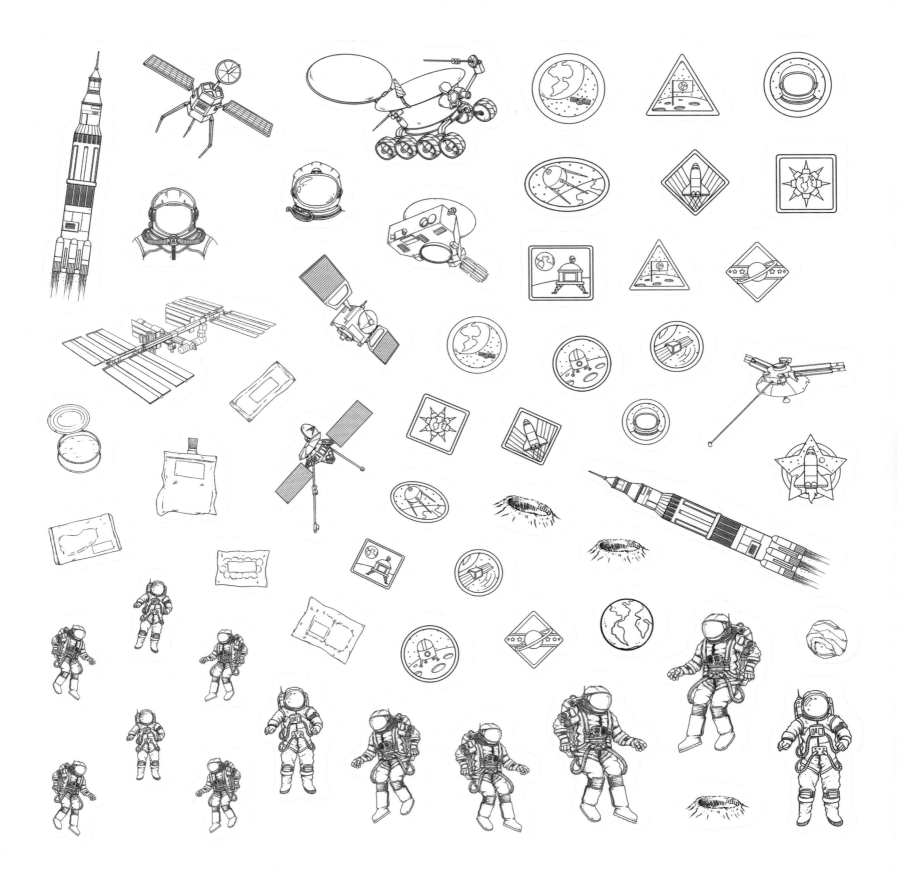